Unique Australia

Unique Australia

Our landscapes, plants and wildlife

Geoff Higgins and Dianne Norris

CHILD & ASSOCIATES
AN ALL-AUSTRALIAN PUBLISHER

We Would Especially Like to Thank

Mr Jim Stopford (herpetologist), Wilmont, NSW
Mr Gerry Walsh (native orchid grower), Werrington, NSW
Featherdale Wildlife Park, Doonside, NSW
NSW Department of Agriculture, Entomology
National Parks and Wildlife Service in each State
The Australian Museum, NSW, department of herpetology and ornithology
Royal Botanic Gardens, Sydney, NSW
Taronga Park Zoo, NSW

Published by
Child & Associates Publishing Pty Ltd,
9 Clearview Place, Brookvale, NSW, Australia, 2100
A wholly owned Australian publishing company
This book has been edited and designed in Australia by the publisher.
Co-published in the U.K. and North America by
Merehurst Press, 5 Great James Street, London, WC1N 3DA

First Edition 1987

Text by Dianne Norris
Photographs by Geoff Higgins

Typeset by Deblaere and Associates
Printed in Australia by Owen King Printers Pty Ltd

National Library of Australia Cataloguing-in-Publication

ISBN 0 86777 322 7.

1. Botany – Australia – Pictorial works. 2. Botany – Australia. 3. Zoology – Australia – Pictorial works. 4. Zoology – Australia. I. Norris, Dianne. II. Title.

574.994

Half-title: One of the attractive *Litoria* species (see page 141).

Title: Rainforest Fungi (see page 107).

Right: King Parrot
Copious in the densely forested mountain ranges of the east coast from Queensland down to south-western Victoria, the handsome king parrot (*Alisterus scapularis*) nests from October to January in a large cavity in a trunk or branch of a tall eucalypt. Often feeding in pairs or in small groups, their diet consists primarily of seeds, berries, fruits, nuts, nectar, blossoms and buds.

Contents

Kakadu National Park (Above)

The inclusion of Stage 2 in 1983 increased the size of Kakadu National Park, in the Northern Territory, to 1.3 million ha. Encompassing Arnhem Land from the floodplains of the Alligator River to the mangrove swamps of Van Diemen Gulf, an inconceivable array of landscapes and wildlife abounds. There are some 1000 plant species, 300 different kinds of birds, 75 types of reptiles and about 50 mammal species living in the rocky escarpments, in and along the endless rivers and wetlands and throughout the entire expanse of this natural phenomenon. Apart from preserving the Aborigines' culture, Kakadu offers its many visitors solitude and breathtaking scenery which is truly unique.

Introduction

Australia is a unique island continent blessed with remarkable landscapes and unequalled flora and fauna. From lush rainforests, along endless beaches and rocky shores, to alpine forests and into the arid desert centre, Australia's diversity and splendour is incomparable.

At one time every landmass on earth was joined together forming one immense continent called Pangaea. About 200 million years ago this vast land divided forming two super-continents—Laurasia in the north and Gondwanaland in the south. Australia was part of Gondwanaland which included landmasses now recognised as South America, Africa, Madagascar, India and New Zealand. Around 55 million years ago, Australia became totally separated. It is still moving southwards at a rate of about seven centimetres per year.

Being the largest island on earth and the smallest continent with an area of 7 682 300 square kilometres, Australia occupies about 5.7 per cent of the world's land surface (excluding Antarctica). Our country is relatively flat—the average altitude being only 300 metres. The highest point is Mt Kosciusko (New South Wales), at 2228 metres and the lowest point is Lake Eyre (South Australia), at 15 metres below sea level.

Australia is made up of six States—New South Wales, Victoria, Tasmania, South Australia, Western Australia and Queensland; and two Territories—the Northern Territory and the Australian Capital Territory. The largest of these is Western Australia with an area of 2 525 500 square kilometres and Tasmania is the smallest being 67 800 square kilometres. Australia also administers the surrounding islands of Lord Howe (part of New South Wales), Norfolk, Christmas, Cocos, Heard, McDonald, Coral Sea, Ashmore and Cartier Islands as well as a large part of Antarctica, called the Australian Antarctic Territory.

The climate is generally warm as two-fifths of the country lies north of the Tropic of Capricorn. The size of the continent rather than its relatively flat topography dictates climatic conditions, therefore the highest temperatures and driest areas are in the centre. Likewise, the ocean modifies temperatures, so most coastal areas are cooled and moistened by sea-breezes.

Australia is the driest continent on earth (again excluding Antarctica) with an average rainfall of less than 300 mm a year—almost one-third of the land has less than 200 mm per annum. The driest area is around the salt lakes east of Lake Eyre in South Australia which receives the lowest average of 100 mm. The highest rainfall areas are along the east coast of Queensland—at Tully the average yearly rainfall is about 4300 mm. High rainfalls are also apparent in the Snowy Mountains and western Tasmania. Snow falls regularly on the Australian Alps above 1500 metres altitude and on the Tasmanian highlands above 1200 metres.

Australia is unique primarily because of its isolation as a continent. During the continental shift this land became disconnected from other landmasses, surrounded by oceans and continued to evolve alone. New Guinea, which was once part of the same continental mass, is our nearest neighbour, situated 139 km to the north. It shares many of our wildlife species.

Unique Australia is an informative visual introduction to some of the many exceptional features abounding in Australia. We have carefully selected some of the most interesting and accessible areas as well as the more remote regions that house our wonderful assortment of flora and fauna. Australia boasts some 252 species of mammals, 750 species of birds, around 530 species of reptiles, 188 species of amphibians, and more than 55 000 species of insects. And of course we have an incredible variety of flora—plants, flowers and trees. These are represented here in the colour photographs and the descriptive text.

Australia is an ancient land, remote and fascinating. To the many people who are familiar with our land and to the many beyond her shores who want to see and know more, this book will serve as a useful companion. This volume has been compiled to answer questions and introduce you to many of the marvellous attributes that make up *Unique Australia.*

Landscapes

The Australian continent covers 7 682 300 square kilometres and is the oldest landmass on earth. Weatherbeaten and worn over millions of years, the landscape has been moulded into one of splendour and uniqueness. The amazing monolith Ayers Rock epitomises this.

Throughout this land extends diversified geographical features and natural wonders, from the ancient volcanic plugs of the Warrumbungles in New South Wales, to petrified forests, through extensive gorges and valleys, into the open vastness of the desert interior, along countless rocky shores and beautiful beaches to the tropical, unspoiled islands off the Queensland coast.

Many outstanding areas have been set aside and secured as national parks. These have been established and maintained under State Government and Federal control for various reasons—scientific research, education, protection of wildlife and their habitats, to preserve scenery and historic sites, to provide a wide range of recreational activities such as boating, camping, hiking, birdwatching and also to safeguard ancient and sacred Aboriginal spiritual and art sites. Once a national park has been declared, it is cared for by such bodies as the National Parks and Wildlife Service and dedicated nature enthusiasts.

However only 4 per cent of our total landmass has been enveloped in this manner, so many splendid and scenic wonders lie outside the confines of these established areas. Kilometres of rocky coastline, beaches and foreshores are considered no-man's-land but are still a significant part of Australia's panoramic appeal. So too are many inland regions.

The beautiful photographs and informative descriptions that follow cover the more popular and familiar attractions such as Ayers Rock, the Great Barrier Reef and the Blue Mountains, as well as the infrequented expanses of the outback, the often inaccessible tracts of far northern Australia and the forgotten corners of this magnificent land.

Fraser Island (Left)
Fraser Island just off Maryborough, Queensland, is the world's largest sand island, being some 120 km long and about 22 km wide. It also encompasses the world's greatest cluster of perched lakes, which are permanent rain lakes formed above sea level. This magnificent island embraces an incredible array of landscapes, from rainforests to mangrove swamps, crystal clear lakes, unspoiled sandcliffs and surf beaches. A focal point is the east coast where massive sandcliffs, weathered over time, boast a multitude of different grain colours.

Sphinx Rocks (Above)
Incorporating a section of the Great Dividing Range just inside the Queensland border, the 11 300 ha Girraween National Park houses massive granite boulders, such as these Sphinx Rocks that balance perilously upon each other, as well as spectacular gullies and gorges carved by years of erosion and dissected by uninterrupted creeks.

Lady Elliott Island (Left and above)
Basking in the magnificent coral wonder of the Great Barrier Reef, Lady Elliott Island, north-east of Bundaberg, Queensland, is a popular tourist destination offering a paradise for the sunloving traveller.

Jourama National Park (Above left)
Jourama National Park is a 1070 ha reserve about 35 km south of Ingham, Queensland. A host of waterfalls, in particular the breathtaking Jourama Falls, cascade over salmon-coloured granite bolders amid lush vegetation including eucalypt forests and rainforest.

Carnarvon Gorge National Park (Left)
In the central highlands sandstone belt of Queensland, a deep, winding gorge has been carved over thousands of years by the Comet and Fitzroy Rivers. Carnarvon Gorge National Park is an area of some 28 500 ha which encompasses mighty sandstone cliffs, narrow ravines with damp, moss-covered walls and chiselled rock pools forming a fertile oasis in these dry highland plains. Within this moist haven, the Moss Gardens flourish and are a major attraction.

Millaa Millaa Falls (Above)
A fine example of our scenic countryside, the Atherton Tableland in north Queensland are remnants of volcanic eruptions from millions of years past. Deep crater lakes and hills of old basaltic volcanoes and cinder-cones form the present geography of this outstanding region. Millaa Millaa Falls tumble effortlessly within a rainforest into one of these cavities created aeons ago.

Kosciusko National Park (Above left)
Kosciusko National Park is the largest park in New South Wales, covering some 690 000 ha of the southern area. At 2228 metres, Mt Kosciusko is the highest point in Australia and is surrounded by the other peaks of Twynam, Townsend and Carruthers. Serene mountain lakes—Blue, Albina, Cootapatamba and Club—are outstanding scenic attractions of this alpine region. Winter snow attracts thousands of skiing enthusiasts each season and the summer months provide ecstasy for avid bushwalkers when the exposed landscape is carpeted with beautiful flowers.

Weeping Rock (Left)
The Blue Mountains National Park in New South Wales covers over 200 000 ha of rocky sandstone plateaux, deep gorges and forested valleys of the Great Dividing Range. Dramatic waterfalls, such as this one at Weeping Rock, tumble effortlessly into the gorges even during the drier periods of the year.

Three Sisters (Above)
The Three Sisters, jagged rock formations overlooking the Jamieson Valley, New South Wales, are spectacular highlights of the panoramic plateaux around Katoomba, situated only 106 km west of Sydney.

Royal National Park (Below)
Majestic Wattamolla Falls are just a small attraction of the 15 014 ha Royal National Park located 36 km south of Sydney. This is Australia's oldest national park, gazetted in 1879, and was the second such reserved area in the world behind America's Yellowstone National Park. An inexhaustible array of diverse scenery and geography—coastal beaches, rivers, tumbling waterfalls, towering cliffs, sandstone plateaux, heathland, densely vegetated valleys—provide a haven for wildlife and activities such as swimming, canoeing, picnicking, bushwalking and birdwatching.

Ben Boyd National Park (Right)
Skirting either side of Twofold Bay near Eden on the south-east coast of New South Wales, Ben Boyd National Park is a 9000 ha site that envelopes the rocky coastline. The park is highlighted with staggering cliffs, rugged outcrops, unblemished beaches and heathland. From Long Beach, the Pinnacles, a colourful and craggy rock formation composed on layers of folded sandstone and shale, is an outstanding feature.

Kanangra Walls (Below right)
About 180 km west of Sydney is situated the rugged wilderness of the Blue Mountains. Kanangra–Boyd National Park is within this spectacular region where masses of waterfalls cascade from the craggy plateau into the Kanangra Gorge. Unspoiled, this environment is a haven for nature buffs.

Lord Howe Island (Above)
One of the most beautifully scenic and unspoiled islands in the world lolls in the Pacific Ocean just 790 km from Sydney. Lord Howe Island is a drop of paradise. Only 12 km in length and from 0.75 to 2 km wide, wooded hills, crystal clear lagoons, perfect beaches, sea meadows, palm groves and a marine wonderland have confirmed this island's standing on the World Heritage listing. Mt Gower at 866 metres and Mt Lidgbird at 765 metres dominate the isle and interestingly, Mt Gower's summit is vegetated in gnarled and mossy rainforest. Lord Howe Island is home to numerous seabirds and one of the rarest birds living today, the woodhen.

Warrumbungle National Park (Left)
The 19 896 ha Warrumbungle National Park was established in 1953 and is 35 km from Coonabarrabran in New South Wales. More than 13 million years ago this area was an active volcanic region, now only remnants form barren spires, excavated ravines and forested ridges. Most impressive is the incredible 90 metre high wall—the Breadknife.

Wombeyan Caves (Right)
Incredible stalagmites, stalactites, coloured stones and frozen rock formations adorn the ancient limestone Wombeyan Caves just 64 km west of Mittagong in New South Wales. Situated on the tranquil Wollondilly River, a huge and picturesque bushland reserve surrounds these spectacular caves.

Port Campbell National Park (Above and right)
Sculptured by wild winds and raging storms that lash the Victorian coast, a rugged series of gorges, arches, blowholes and islands form the astounding national park of Port Campbell. Two of the best known highlights are the Twelve Apostles and London Bridge.

Wilsons Promontory National Park (Left)
Covering the most southerly part of the Australian mainland, 130 km of magnificent coastline form Wilsons Promontory National Park. It is Victoria's largest and most popular national park encompassing 49 000 ha of superior coastal scenery—unspoiled beaches, granite ranges, tall forests, heathlands and an enormous array of wildlife. Squeaky Beach nature walk is a favourite.

Petrified Forest (Above left)
A few kilometres from Portland, Victoria, is an unusual and extraordinary forest. This petrified forest is actually a series of tree trunks that have been fossilised thousands of years ago.

Organ Pipes National Park (Left)
Resembling the musical instrument after which they were named, the colossal basalt pillars of the Organ Pipes National Park are the central feature of this 85 ha Victorian region located just 25 km north-west of Melbourne.

Cyathea Falls (Above)
The beautifully cascading Cyathea Falls are a highlight of the 140 ha Tarra Valley National Park, 35 km south of Traralgon in Victoria. Lush rainforest shelters numerous waterfalls, walking tracks and a treasure-chest of lavish flora.

Cradle Mountain – Lake St Clair National Park (Left)
A vast wilderness in western Tasmania of alpine and mountainous country is captured in the unsurpassed Cradle Mountain–Lake St Clair National Park. Here Tasmania's highest peak, Mt Ossa stands at 1617 metres in the centre of the reserve. Lake St Clair is the deepest lake—a staggering 200 metres. This incredibly scenic and unspoiled wilderness region is of such significant beauty and uniqueness as to be inscribed onto the World Heritage listing.

Lake Pedder (Below left)
Situated in the rugged south-west region of Tasmania, on the Serpentine River, a tributary of the now famous Gordon River, Lake Pedder was formerly a lake naturally dammed within this glacial valley. Magnificent shorelines and unequalled beaches have vanished forever under the risen water level which was created by the construction of three hydro-electric dams, signifying perhaps one of the worst environmental disasters of recent times.

Freycinet National Park (Below)
Picturesque Honeymoon Bay is just one of the many unspoiled white sandy beaches found in the Freycinet National Park on the east coast of Tasmania. This 10 010 ha reserve embraces Freycinet Peninsula and Shouten Island where many scenic bays, rock pools, offshore islands and coastal heathlands, alive with spring wildflowers and birdlife, can be enjoyed.

Port Arthur and Remarkable Cave (Above and above right)
Between 1830 and 1877 Port Arthur, on the southern boundary of the Tasman Peninsula, was the penal establishment of Tasmania, then known as Van Diemen's Land. Apart from the interesting historic ruins and sites, intriguing networks of caves are highlights of this area.

St Columba Falls State Reserve (Right)
St Columba Falls is a Tasmanian State Reserve covering some 314 ha in the north-east region. Picnicking and walking tracks to these impressive falls are of interest to the visitor.

Tessellated Pavement State Reserve (Above)
Unusual and spectacular, the Tessellated Pavement State Reserve at Eaglehawk Neck in Tasmania forms a meagre isthmus separating the Tasman Sea from the Forester Peninsula.

Flinders Chase National Park (Right, above and below)
Almost the entire western side of Kangaroo Island girdles the 73 103 ha Flinders Chase National Park. This, Australia's second-largest island, lies 14.5 km from the South Australian mainland and embraces densely foliaged sandhills in the south rising to richly forested highland sectors in the north. The Remarkable Rocks are sculptured masterpieces, shaped and fashioned over many years by the tempestuous elements. Admiralty Arch, below the stalactite escarpment of Cape de Couedic, is a breathtaking feature.

Coober Pedy (Above)
Excessively hot and dry, the opal-mining settlement of Coober Pedy was established in 1911. Located in the arid centre of South Australia, some 931 km north-west of Adelaide, this desolate area has an Aboriginal name meaning 'hole in the ground'. Many people who live here make their homes in dugouts underground to beat the extreme climate.

Flinders Ranges National Park (Left)
The sprawling 80 265 ha Flinders Ranges National Park, 350 km north of Adelaide, unites much of the grassy plains, creeks, gorges and rugged mountains of the Flinders Ranges. An exuberant wealth of wildlife and flora thrives here providing an absolute sanctum for nature enthusiasts.

(Right)
Mount Billy Creek within Wilkawillana Gorge, South Australia.

Mt Remarkable National Park (Above)
At 995 metres, Mt Remarkable is the highest point of the 8600 ha Mt Remarkable National Park which lies 270 km north of Adelaide. Craggy, weather-beaten cliffs tower over the peaceful streams that meander through this thickly wooded expanse of the southern Flinders Ranges. Here the spectacular high cliff of the Battery Ridge along the Hidden Gorge trail gives a taste of this impressive area.

Torndirrup National Park (Right)
Panoramic seascapes of the untamed coastline south-west of Albany in Western Australia are encased in the 3870 ha Torndirrup National Park. A labyrinth of gulfs, gorges, cliffs, blowholes, rocky headlands, beaches and breathtaking scenery is guarded by Bald Head, the most easterly aspect of the cape.

Kalbarri National Park (Above left)
The swift, powerful flow of the Murchison River has carved a deep passage through the sandplains 155 km north of Geraldton in Western Australia, creating a trail of multi-coloured rocky gorges that watch this river's journey to the Indian Ocean. Kalbarri National Park is a 186 076 ha guardian of these spectacular ravines and gorges that encompass the culmination of this river's trek.

Eucla National Park (Left)
Near Esperance on the West Australian and South Australian border, clean, white, distinctive sand formations and patterns on the sand-dunes are the focal point of the 3342 ha Eucla National Park. Some mallee scrub grows here and exciting views of the Great Australian Bight can be enjoyed.

The Pinnacles (Above)
Standing proudly and abruptly from the coastal plains of Western Australia and protected by Nambung National Park, is this geological phenomenon. Tree roots and trunks, which once secured the sand-dunes, have transformed over millions of years, becoming petrified into calcified limestone pillars, some as high as 6 metres. The majority of the 17 487 ha park is sand-dune opening into low woodlands and scrub.

Stirling Range National Park (Above)
Rising abruptly from the lush farmland belt of south-western Australia, the rocky mountains of the Stirling Range are captured in the 115 671 ha Stirling Range National Park. An outstounding diversity of wildflowers blooms throughout all seasons offering unparalleled walking excursions and scenery.

Windjana Gorge (Left)
During the wet season when the Lennard River is in full flood, the 2100 ha Napier Range National Park in Western Australia becomes inaccessible. Jagged limestone walls of the narrow Windjana Gorge often tower as high as 90 metres and woodlands with tropical fig species thrive within the crannies of the extensively weathered rock chasms.

Ayers Rock (Right)
Probably the most notable landmark in Australia is the world's largest monolith (single rock), Ayers Rock, situated in the centre of the continent within Uluru National Park, Northern Territory. Composed of hard-rock conglomerate, it is 8.8 km in circumference, 3.6 km long, 2.5 km wide and reaches some 348 metres in height. A popular tourist destination, this spectacular feature has important ritual and mythological significance to the Aborigines.

Kings Canyon National Park (Above)
Established in 1984, the 76 000 ha Kings Canyon National Park is a splendid example of the overall grandeur of the Northern Territory's terrain. Deep gorges rising about 200 metres have been carved by ancient rivers but now are occupied by Kings Creek and its tributaries. Palms, cycads, figs, ferns and cypress pines are plentiful around these watercourses.

Chambers Pillar (Left)
About 170 km south of Alice Springs in the Northern Terrritory erupts the huge imposing sandstone monolith, Chambers Pillar. This area was established as a national reserve in 1970.

Devils Marbles Conservation Reserve (Right)
The Devils Marbles Conservation Reserve near Wauchope, Northern Territory, is a stark feature rising from the seemingly endless barren plains. Massive granite boulders, some measuring 6 metres in diameter, balance delicately in their desert environment. Sunset, when the rocks glow a deep, burnt orange and vivid red, is the best time of day to marvel at this rare formation.

The Olgas (Left)
Thirty–two km west of Ayers Rock, in the Uluru National Park, Northern Territory another boulder-conglomeration emanates from the desert land. Mt Olga towers some 546 metres above the ground and is the largest in this grouping of dome-like rocks known as the Olgas.

Twin Gums (Below left)
Often painted by such renowned artists as Albert Namatjira, these twin ghost gums withstand the unrelenting conditions of the eastern MacDonnell Ranges, Northern Territory.

Ormiston Gorge and Pound National Park (Right)
Sheer cliffs of multi-coloured quartzite form the red and yellow ridges of Ormiston Gorge and Pound National Park, Northern Territory. Through this canyon, Ormiston Creek lazily wanders. Characteristic of this park are the variegated rocks, numerous rock pools and the shady ghost gums.

Douglas Hot Springs (Below)
On the picturesque Douglas River just a few kilometres from Pine Creek in the Northern Territory, the steamy and inviting Douglas Hot Springs offer a tranquil uninterrupted sanctuary.

Mammals

Some of the most ancient forms of mammals surviving in the world today live in Australia. Mammals first appeared on earth about 195 to 225 million years ago during the Triassic Period. Fossils from that time provide evidence that mammals evolved from reptiles, therefore like birds, they have become 'improved reptiles'.

Of the estimated world total of some 4000 mammal species, 5 to 6 per cent (about 250 species) are native to Australia. Of the seventeen orders of land mammals, four inhabit this vast land—the monotremes, marsupials and placentals. Coastal waters are populated by all three orders of marine mammals—cetaceans (whales and dolphins), seals and dugongs (sea-cows).

Mammals are warm-blooded (homoeothermic) vertebrates—that is, they have a backbone. Having a constant body temperature, usually higher than that of their surroundings, enables mammals to be active even when their environmental temperature is low. Their hair insulates—regulating the body temperature thus inhibiting the loss of body heat in cold temperatures and the gaining of heat in very high temperatures. All mammals suckle their young on milk which the female secretes through mammary glands (breasts or teats) or ducts enabling the offspring to suckle, obtain nourishment and grow.

Monotremes

Monotremes are extraordinary and primitive mammals; only two subgroups are known to exist—the echidna (spiny anteater) and the platypus. The platypus is unique to Australia but the echidna inhabits both Australia and New Guinea.

Female monotremes lay soft-shelled eggs, suckle their young on milk which is discharged through numerous ducts opening onto her abdomen and the young are nurtured in a temporary pouch.

Monotremes have no whiskers, teeth or external ears. The males have a hollow spur on the ankle. In the platypus it is connected to a venom gland, but in the echidna it appears to have no function.

Both monotremes flourish in quite different environments—the echidna lives on land, residing in most areas of the country from cold, snowy regions to the hot desert interior. It feeds on ants, termites and insects. The platypus is an aquatic mammal living in and near rivers and streams along the eastern belt of Australia. It feeds primarily on aquatic invertebrates (animals without a backbone).

Both types of monotremes are quite common and are protected by law.

Marsupials

There are about 120 species of marsupials native to Australia which is regarded as their natural home. The word 'marsupial' derives from the Latin *marsupium* meaning 'pouch'.

The most fascinating feature peculiar to marsupials is their method of reproduction. Females give birth to their young in an embryonic state—very immature, small and naked. However, each infant is exceptionally well developed in its forelimbs, enabling it to climb up the hair of its mother towards her external pouch in which it attaches itself to the teat, suckles and completes its development.

When the young reaches a certain stage of growth, about equivalent to that of a placental mammal at birth, it will emerge from the pouch returning frequently to feed.

Most marsupials are insect- or plant-eating but some, like the quolls, dunnarts and marsupial moles are carnivorous, eating small mammals or birds.

This large group of Australian mammals includes the koalas, wombats, possums, kangaroos and wallabies.

Placentals

This group is neither monotreme nor marsupial. Placental mammals have proved to be the most successful mammals, a fact attributed to their larger and more efficient brain and their favourable method of reproduction. Female placentals produce young which are more advanced at birth than those of marsupials; nurturing the unborn embryo so it is well developed at birth. The foetus is nourished by means of the placenta—a vascular organ in the uterus of the female that during pregnancy provides oxygen and nutrients to the growing infant.

This large group includes bats, rats, mice, seals and of course human beings.

Koala (Left and above)

An accomplished climber, this tail-less, arboreal marsupial (*Phascolarctos cinereus*) is one of our most esteemed inhabitants. Sleeping peacefully during the day, it feeds after sunset and throughout the night. Koalas are limited to south-eastern Australia where particular types of eucalypts are available as a food supply; they eat the foliage which is also high in water content thus they rarely drink. These adorable animals are fully protected by law and their survival depends on the maintenance and protection of their environment.

Feathertail Glider (Above)
Feasting on nectar, sugary sap, blossoms or small insects, the feathertail glider (*Acrobates pygmaeus*) is a common marsupial found throughout wet eucalypt forests of the east coast. A membrane from elbow to knee allows this tiny creature to glide up to 20 metres in one go. The flattened, feathery tail acts as a steering implement as well as a brake and anchorage to branches. Mostly nocturnal, these gliders are dormant during the day.

Common Brushtail Possum (Above right)
Familiar and plentiful, the common brushtail possum (*Trichosurus vulpecula*) frequents areas of open forest and woodland—wherever there are trees. Like most possums, this marsupial is nocturnal, spending nights feeding on fruits, buds and leaves and finding refuge in a hollow log, branch or tree trunk during the day. Brushtail possums are friendly, if unprovoked, and often occupy domestic buildings.

Eastern Grey Kangaroo (Right)
Unlike other large kangaroos, the eastern grey kangaroo (*Macropus giganteus*) has a hairy muzzle. Abundant throughout the semi-arid scrubland, woodland and forested regions on the eastern side of the continent, this marsupial rests in the shade during the daytime and grazes on grasses at night. Its peak breeding season is summer.

Red Kangaroo (Left)
One of the largest living marsupials of Australia, the familiar red kangaroo (*Macropus rufus*) prefers the open plains, shrubby grasslands, and desert regions of the continent's interior. Not all red kangaroos are red; usually the females verge on a blue-grey colour. Like most other dwellers of the hot, arid centre, they rest during the heat of the day and spend the cool nights grazing on grasses and plants.

Red-Necked Wallaby (Below left)
Often called Bennett's Wallaby, the red-necked wallaby (*Macropus rufogriseus*) is abundant in forest regions of the south-eastern part of the country including Tasmania and the larger islands in Bass Strait. This marsupial is generally nocturnal, feeding on herbs and grasses at night. As the young develops, it remains in the pouch for about forty weeks.

Dingo (Right and below)
Common throughout Australia, except Tasmania, the handsome dingo (*Canis familiaris dingo*) was thought to have been introduced into our land by the Aborigines. Often considered a pest, the longest fence in the world has been erected in an attempt to keep this dog out of eastern and southern sheep-grazing land. However, 60 per cent of the dingo's diet consists of small mammals and the remainder of reptiles, birds, rodents and rabbits.

Short-Beaked Echidna (Above)
Abundant throughout the entire continent, the timid and reclusive short-beaked echidna (*Tachyglossus aculeatus*) is one of only two monotremes found living in the world today. Often called the spiny anteater, this little mammal's upper body is protected with long, sharp spines; underneath the body is covered with coarse hair and bristles. At the end of its long, sensitive snout the echidna has a small mouth from which a long, extensile tongue darts out to lap up its favourite food—termites. Echidnas vary in colour from light brown to black, they have a poor sense of sight but this is compensated for by acute hearing. During the breeding months, the female usually lays only one egg from which the young emerges after about ten days then develops within its mother's pouch for another three months.

Tasmanian Devil (Above left)
The largest carnivorous marsupial is the Tasmanian devil (*Sarcophilus harrisii*) and it is only found in Tasmania. Being nocturnal, it emerges at night to feed, mainly on carrion—the dead and decaying corpses of animals. Females are smaller than males and the maximum known lifespan is about seven to eight years.

Grey-Headed Flying-Fox (Left)
Hanging comfortably upside down from a tree branch is the grey-headed flying-fox (*Pteropus poliocephalus*), often called a fruit bat, as it feeds on native fruits, blossoms and nectar. Communication between these placental mammals is by sound; a keen sense of sight acts as their navigation tool and food is located by smell. Young flying-foxes can fly when eight to ten weeks old.

Quokka (Above)
Preferring dense, moist environments, the quokka (*Setonix brachyurus*) is limited to the south-west corner of Western Australia and Rottnest Island. About the size of a domestic cat, this rat-like marsupial breeds throughout most of the year and is quite common within its habitat.

Australian Sea-Lion (Left)
Basking and lolling on the offshore islands from Houtman Abrolhos in Western Australia across to Kangaroo Island off South Australia is the magnificent Australian sea-lion (*Neophoca cinerea*). Male sea-lions are dark black or brown while the females are an attractive silver-grey colour. Only 3000 to 5000 sea-lions are alive today and both males and females are extremely protective and territorial during the breeding season.

Platypus (Above)
Shy and timid, the unique platypus (*Ornithorhynchus anatinus*) is one of only two monotremes alive on earth today. Restricted to the eastern zone of Australia from Cooktown in Queensland into New South Wales, South Australia and Tasmania, its preferred habitat is in deep river pools near which it excavates a maze of tunnels and chambers into the steep earth banks. Essentially nocturnal, this superb little mammal grows to about 45 to 61 cm in length, it has a body covering of short, water-resistant fur, webbed feet which provide agility in the water and a unique beak-like muzzle which is covered with a thin film of skin. Its flattened tail acts as a rudder. An abundant food supply of small vertebrates is readily available in its aquatic environment. Females breed during spring laying one to three leathery eggs in the security of the nursery chamber which is lined with grasses and leaves. Incubation takes about ten days. The platypus is one of our most treasured assets and is strictly protected by law.

Water Buffalo (Above)
This imposing perhaps menacing animal is the huge water buffalo (*Bubalus bubalis*) which was thought to have been introduced into Australia from Indonesia between 1825 and 1843. It roams as a feral intruder throughout its very limited range of the northern sector of the Northern Territory, where it grazes on aquatic and terrestrial plants.

Bilby (Left)
Restricted to the desert regions of Central Australia and a few scattered colonies in the Kimberleys and Warburton areas of Western Australia, one of our rarest marsupials is the bilby (*Macrotis lagotis*). Being nocturnal in habit, it spends the hot daylight hours deep in its underground burrow emerging well after dark to feed on insects, larvae, seeds, bulbs, fruit and fungi found around the hummock grasslands and acacia shrublands in which it lives.

Common Wombat (Above and right)
Common, stout and large, these incredible herbivorous marsupials (*Vombatus ursinus*) inhabit forest-covered sectors of south-eastern Australia, often in the more mountainous pockets. Cumbersome and often weighing up to 40 kg, wombats excavate enormous, intricate burrows with several entrances leading to an underground maze of tunnels and chambers. Here they reside during the hotter days, emerging at dusk to feed on native grasses, sedges, mat-rushes and plant roots. Usually only one offspring is raised during the breeding time and remains in its mother's pouch for six months.

Bush Rat (Above)
Being nocturnal, the bush rat (*Rattus fuscipes*) is rarely observed in its natural habitats of subalpine woodlands, coastal forests and rainforests where it flourishes amongst the thick ground foliage. It feeds by night on insects and occasionally plant material. Breeding throughout the year, these abundant little placental mammals usually bear five live young per litter. At birth they weigh a mere five grams but quickly grow and become independent at four to five weeks of age.

Kowari (Above left)
The shy and reclusive kowari (*Dasyuroides byrnei*) is often called the brushtailed marsupial rat. Inhabiting the sparse and desolate gibber deserts of south-western Queensland, this little marsupial feasts on a wide array of insects, carrion and small vertebrates. Kowaris breed between May and December and six young are usually raised.

Brown Antechinus (Left)
This cute, mouse-like little marsupial is the brown antechinus (*Antechinus stuartii*). Dwelling in the forested regions of south-eastern Australia these carnivorous animals dine on beetles, spiders and cockroaches. It is interesting to note that the male of the species dies when only 46 weeks of age after a few brief days of mating. Females, however, usually survive until the following breeding season.

Water Rat (Right)
With partially webbed hind feet and waterproof fur, the water rat (*Hydromys chrysogaster*) has adapted splendidly to its aquatic environment. Tunnels are excavated into riverbanks at the end of which a comfortable nest is made. Here the female breeds up to five times throughout spring and summer, usually bearing three to four young per litter. Always dwelling near permanent bodies of water, a plentiful food supply of fish, large aquatic insects and crustaceans is readily available.

Spotted-Tailed Quoll (Above)
One of our largest carnivorous marsupials is the spotted-tailed quoll (*Dasyurus maculatus*). Even though it is an agile and expert climber, it spends most of its time searching the forest floor for food—rodents, birds, small mammals and reptiles. It is rare in its restricted range of sclerophyll forests and rainforests on the east coastal edge, due to competition with the fox and feral cat, as well as the fact that its habitat is being cleared for agricultural land. The spotted-tailed quoll, often called the tiger quoll, has been described as the most ferocious Australian bush inhabitant.

Eastern Quoll (Left)
Perhaps better known as the native cat, the eastern quoll (*Dasyurus viverrinus*) is quite common throughout Tasmania, but is very rare on the mainland. Attractively coloured with black or brown fur enhanced with white spots, these marsupials are basically carnivorous, eating a selection of insects, grubs, ground-dwelling birds, rodents and sometimes vegetation. Inhabiting the dry sclerophyll forests, scrubland, heathland and agricultural belts, they reside in dens such as underground burrows, hollow tree logs or rock piles.

Northern Brown Bandicoot (Right)
Preferring low-foliaged areas within grasslands, woodlands and open forests, the northern brown bandicoot (*Isoodon macrourus*) thrives in the higher rainfall areas across northern Western Australia, the Northern Territory, Queensland and down to central New South Wales. Being nocturnal, this little marsupial feasts on insects, spiders, earthworms and plant foliage during the cooler evening hours. Males are larger and more aggressive than the females who rear a litter of one to seven infants.

Brush-Tailed Phascogale (Left)

Retiring during the day to the comfort of its nest formed in the hollow of a tree, the charming little brush-tailed phascogale (*Phascogale tapoatafa*) emerges at dusk to feast mainly on arthropods—spiders and centipedes. With long, sharp claws it is arboreal, living among the trees of open dry sclerophyll forests. Like other members of its genus, the male brush-tailed phascogale has an unusual breeding pattern. At the end of its very first and brief breeding season, it mates then promptly dies. The female however usually survives to breed the following year.

Sugar Glider (Right)

Able to spread the membrane in each side of its body and volplane up to 50 metres or more, the enchanting little sugar glider (*Petaurus breviceps*) only grows to about 170 mm. Abundant in its favourite habitat of open coastal forests where there are plenty of acacia trees, it eats gum and sap as well as insects. These social marsupials often live in small groups. The breeding season starts in August and each female usually bears two offspring which remain in her pouch for seventy days.

Squirrel Glider (Below)

This scarce squirrel glider (*Petaurus norfolcensis*) is the same in appearance and habits as the sugar glider except it is almost twice the size. Being restricted to the dry sclerophyll forests and woodland regions of the eastern side of Australia it is a rare marsupial whose existence is under constant threat as more of its habitat is cleared for farmland.

Insects and Spiders

Insects

The world of insects is intricate and fascinating. Can you imagine a world devoid of insects? It would be quite hard to do since they are the largest class of animals existing—almost one million species. Five-sixths of the known animal life are insects and it is quite possible that these figures only represent one-third of what yet is to be scientifically described. There are between 55 000 and 56 000 known insect species in Australia.

An insect is any invertebrate animal that has wings although not all insects have wings. All have segmented bodies, that is they have three body regions: the head, which contains mouthparts, eyes and a pair of antennae or feelers; the thorax, usually sprouting three pairs of legs and one or two pairs of wings; and the abdomen, where the digestive, excretory and reproductive organs are found. Insects have jointed legs and when present, a hard external skeleton (exoskeleton).

Most insects are small (less than 6 mm in length) and this, along with their high rate of reproduction and abundance of food, contributes to their very large population. They have successfully adapted to every land and water habitat where food is plentiful; deserts, jungles, mountains, forests and glacial fields.

Insects play important roles in nature. They assist bacteria, fungi and other organisms in decomposing organic matter and in soil formation. They also pollinate many flowers, therefore it is reasonable to conclude that flowers and insects have evolved virtually simultaneously. The oldest insect fossils date back some 350 million years.

Apart from their invaluable assistance to nature, man also benefits from and exploits commercial products from insects—like honey, wax, silk, dyes and pigments. Insects also provide food for some native peoples—our Aborigines include witchetty grubs on their menu.

Most insects begin life as a fertilized egg; nymphs or larvae hatch from these and develop into a pupa, which finally emerges from its cocoon as an adult. Their diet consists of plant material, decaying organic matter and parasites on other animals. Some insects are cannibalistic predators, capturing and eating their fellow insects.

The largest orders of insects in Australia include the beetles, butterflies, moths, ants, bees, wasps and flies.

Spiders

Of the 34 000 species of spiders so far described living on earth today, 1400 species are known to exist in Australia, but obviously, many more are yet to be discovered.

Spiders have a body divided into two segments—a combined head and thorax and an abdomen—unlike the three body parts that insects possess. They have eight legs whereas insects have only six. All spiders have a keen sense of sight.

They feed mainly on insects which often fly through and become captured in the silken webs which they weave. Webs can be very complex and elaborate works of art but not all spiders construct them or catch food in this manner. The Australian trapdoor digs a burrow in the soil, lidded with a saucer-shaped trapdoor. The notorious funnel web also retreats into its nest in the ground but instead of a trapdoor a white, silky web covers the opening. Many, like the Australian red-back, inject venom into their prey—paralysing and killing it.

Spiders often bring out our worst fears but most are quite harmless. However, the Sydney funnel web is extremely common in and around that city and can cause death to humans. The male is more venomous than the female and will attack readily if interfered with or threatened. The red-back spider is not as aggressive but if accidently squeezed will inject a poisonous but non-fatal venom. The male of this species is thought to be non-venomous. If bitten by a spider medical attention should be sought immediately as an effective antivenene is readily available.

Common Jezebel Butterfly (Left)
One of our largest families of butterflies includes the attractive common jezebel butterfly (*Delias nigrina*). Ranging from Cape York in far northern Queensland down to the southern regions of New South Wales, these slow-flying insects are quite common and this female of the species is more colourful than the male.

Wanderer or Monarch Butterfly (Below)
Conspicuous throughout most of our country excluding Tasmania and Western Australia, the strikingly designed wanderer or monarch butterfly (*Danaus plexippus*) is a descendant of the well-known North American species which is famous for its annual migration. These attractive insects are very robust and are often seen congregating in their thousands.

Orchard Swallowtail Butterfly (Left and above)
Common in their range from Cape York right down to eastern Victoria, the beautiful orchard swallowtail butterfly (*Papilio aegeus aegeus*) is so named because one of its favourite haunts is around young citrus orchards. Even though the male (left) is quite attractive, it is the female (above) which is more colourfully and elaborately patterned.

Chequered Swallowtail Butterfly (Right)
Beautifully coloured and patterned, the chequered swallowtail butterfly (*Papilio demoleus sthenelus*) dwells on mainland Australia only and is especially abundant in northern Queensland. Here is the female; while still gorgeous she is not as ornate as the male but both are amongst the swiftest flying butterflies.

Richmond Birdwing Butterfly (Above)
The family of birdwing butterflies contains some of the largest insects known to exist. This is a beautiful female Richmond birdwing (*Ornithoptera richmondia*).

Blue Triangle Butterfly (Left)
The distinctive iridescent blue of the blue triangle butterfly (*Graphium sarpedon choredon*) ensures that it is one of the most easily recognised and best known of our butterflies. This is the female, and like the male she is a fast flyer often being very elusive.

Orange Lacewing Butterfly (Right)
Intricately patterned and coloured, the orange lacewing (*Cethosia penthesilea paksha*) flourishes throughout the Northern Territory.

Common Brown Moth (Above)
Some moths are quite attractive, like the beautiful female common brown moth (*Heteronympna merope*).

Wood Moth (Right)
Another exponent of camouflage, the wood moth (*Ptilomacra senex*) looks just like a tuft of plant or tree residue.

Ulysses Butterfly (Above left)
Hiding its spectacular blue upper wings, here resting is a Ulysses butterfly (*Papilio ulysses joesa*) found from Cape York to Mackay in Queensland.

Privet Hawk Moth (Left)
A master of camouflage, the privet hawk moth (*Psilogramma menephron*) expertly blends into the colouring and texture of tree bark where it can rest unnoticed.

Orbweaving Spider (Left and below)
The orbweaving spider (*Araneus* sp.) is one of at least 1300 species 'ordinary' spiders found in Australia today. Orbweavers build remarkably strong webs, often constructed in high or windy places.

St Andrew's Cross Spider (Right above and below)
Another of the orbweaving spiders and perhaps the most easily recognised is the St Andrew's cross spider (*Argiope keyserlingi*) so named because of the wide silky web bands shaped in an 'X' across the centre of its web. Here it rests motionless with its legs outstretched along the arms of the cross.

Dragonfly (Above)
Resting with its wings outstretched is the familiar dragonfly (*Diplacodes bipunctata*).

Funnel-Web Spider (Above left)
The notorious funnel-web spider (*Atrax robustus*) is extremely venomous and has caused deaths in humans. A large, dark-coloured spider, the male is more deadly than the female and both attack readily if disturbed or threatened. Very common in the Sydney suburban region, they construct ground holes often in sandstone, crevices, bases of trees or plants and under rubbish. Each entrance is veiled with a white, silky web.

Red-Back Spider (Left)
Thriving in its web safely wedged under rubbish, machinery or any item close to the ground, the attractive yet poisonous red-back spider (*Latrodectus mactans hasselti*) is not aggressive but will bite if accidentally squeezed or interfered with. The female has long, fine legs, and is black with a vivid red mark on her back while the male, which is much smaller, is buff-brown in colour with red or orange markings.

Tree Cricket (Right)
Often feasting on plant foliage and laying its eggs in the slits of tree bark, the common tree cricket (*Paragryllacris* sp.) is only one of at least 700 species of crickets found in Australia.

Purple-Winged Mantid (Left)
Of the some 130 species of mantid living in Australia, the pretty purple-winged mantid (*Tenodera australasiae*) is harmoniously coloured and shaped to blend unnoticed into its habitat.

Stick Insect (Below)
Is this a stick or twig or part of this plant? The mimicking stick insect (*Ctenomorpha* sp.) has perfected camouflage, resembling closely the colour and texture of the twigs from which it feeds. These slow-moving insects most often lack wings and there are some 130 species known throughout our country.

(Right)
This hairy, slow-moving little insect is a member of the Notodontidae family.

Birds

Birds are found in every part of Australia; every environment, every habitat. Australia is renowned for its unique, colourful and diverse birdlife.

Like mammals, birds are 'improved reptiles'. By the Triassic Period, some 225 million years ago, a number of two-footed (bipedal) reptiles existed and it is thought that one of these groups became arboreal—able to live in and among trees. Their forelimbs became modified for flight and the hindlimbs altered enabling perching—thus evolved the bird.

Birds are warm-blooded (homoeothermic) vertebrates, that is they have a constant body temperature of about 41°C. They all have a body covering of feathers, reproduce by hard-shelled eggs and have no teeth. The forelimbs have been modified as wings allowing most to possess the ability to fly. Birds are bipedal animals.

Feathers are unique to birds, providing a light, flat, waterproof insulation to their body. They are made of a fibrous protein called keratin, which is also present in hair and the scales of reptiles. The bill of the bird is also covered with a fine sheet of keratin.

The leg and foot has evolved to suit the environment in which a species lives. For example, birds which walk on aquatic vegetation or soft ground have very long toes, wading birds have very long legs, those which primarily swim have webbed toes and those which climb have developed short legs with strong curved and sharp claws. Birds' feet are covered with scales and are tipped with claws. Most have four toes.

All birds incubate their eggs—meaning that the parent birds provide warmth to the eggs, usually by sitting on them, thus producing heat to allow the infant within the shell to develop until hatching occurs. However some provide incubation in a different way—the megapodes (mound-builders such as the brush turkey or scrub fowl) depend on the heat generated from decaying forest vegetation and others, called 'brood-parasites' avoid incubation altogether by laying their eggs in the nests of other species (like the migratory koel which lays its eggs in the nest of the Australian wattlebird).

Depending on the size of the bird and the stage of development that the chick has achieved when hatched, incubation takes between eleven and eighty days. Young, newly hatched birds are called chicks or nestlings until they are able to fly. Until a young bird has its first plumage of true feathers, it is known as a juvenile. After this and until it becomes an adult and breeds it is termed as immature.

Most birds construct nests into which they lay their eggs. Some are simply a depression in the soil or sand, others a deep burrow in the side of a riverbank; some consist of a hole in a rock or tree, while others still are intricately woven hanging baskets. The materials from which nests are manufactured also show great diversity—small stones, dirt, mud, plant foliage, sticks, feathers, and hair. These materials are woven, sewn and held together with mud, spiderwebs or saliva.

Communication between birds is fundamentally achieved through sight and sound. Birds have a poor sense of smell. Their auditory sounds are called 'songs' and are executed for a variety of reasons—during the breeding season to attract a mate, flocking together while feeding, proclaiming their territory, to warn off a predator or another bird and the begging calls of a hungry or distressed infant.

Most birds eat insects, that is they are insectivorous. But some have additional diets, for example, eagles prey on small mammals, waterbirds eat fish and others have a varied diet of plant matter such as buds, seeds, fruit or nectar.

Of the estimated world total of some 8000 to 9000 species of birds, almost 750 species are found in Australia and adjacent waters. Of these about 368 are endemic to our country—that means they are unique and found nowhere else on earth.

Willie Wagtail (Above right)
One of the most familiar of Australian birds is the Willie wagtail (*Rhipidura leucophrys*). This busy, chattering little bird is found everywhere in the country except dense forests or open, barren plains. Often urban parks and gardens become its favourite habitat where a food supply of insects, spiders and worms is plentiful. Willie wagtails breed from June to February laying three to four eggs. A small, neat, cup-shaped nest is constructed on a horizontal branch, often near water.

Superb Blue Wren (Right)
Sharing in the duties of caring for the young is the male superb blue wren (*Malurus cyaneus*). The female wren is brownish in colour with creamy-brown underparts and so too is the male until the breeding season, from September to March, during which his plumage becomes brilliant blue in order to attract females. Also known as fairy wrens, these energetic, petite birds are common throughout south-eastern Australia, living in groups in hedges, brush and shrubby thickets.

Brolga (Above)
With a height of one metre and a wingspan of two metres, the pale grey brolga (*Grus rubicunda*) rates as one of our most stately birds. Brolgas live in lake and swampland areas of coastal Australia, where a diet of sedge tubers and insects is available. They perform a breathtaking *pas de deux*—dancing in pairs with wings half open and shaking, their heads bowing and bobbing. This is staged mostly during the breeding season but seems to be part of their usual repertoire.

Laughing Kookaburra (Left)
Often at dusk a raucous laughing can be heard. This belongs to the largest member of the kingfisher family, the laughing kookaburra (*Dacelo gigas*). These gregarious birds favour woodlands and open forests along the east coast where a food supply of rodents and reptiles is abundant. Kookaburras, who may live for twenty years or more, nest in hollow trunks or branches of large trees where they lay two or three eggs. Their renowned cacophony is performed to clearly define their territory.

Australian Bustard (Right)
The tall and statuesque Australian bustard (*Ardeotis australis*) is a nomadic bird that moves singly or in small flocks generally in open country. Once common throughout the plains, their numbers have declined to such an extent that they are now rarely seen. Cape York Peninsula, the Barkly Tableland and the Kimberleys are the only places in which their populations remain stable.

Spur-Winged Plover (Left)

The unusual masked, spur-winged plover (*Vanellus miles novaehollandiae*) frequents wet grasslands but is also quite content in suburbia, often inhabiting farmland, parks and gardens. Both parents build the simple nest which is merely a depression in the soil lined with grass. Only two days after the chicks have hatched, the parent birds lead them away to the protection of rougher pasture. Plovers are extremely protective of their eggs and young, often dive-bombing and screaming at approaching intruders.

Black Swan (Right)

Western Australia's State emblem, the majestic black swan (*Cygnus atratus*) is often seen surrounded by her grey, downy cygnets. These beautiful waterbirds eat aquatic plants and nearby grasses. They breed throughout most of the year, but mainly from February to May in the north and May to September in the south.

Emu (Below)

The emu (*Dromaius novaehollandiae*) is the second-largest bird living on earth today. Unable to fly, it is an accomplished runner able to reach speeds of some 50 kph. Interestingly, after the female lays her dark green eggs, the male incubates them, then for the next 18 months or so rears the cream-striped chicks. Emus are plentiful throughout mainland Australia, inhabiting diverse regions from the desert to the tropical north to the cold alpine areas but they tend to avoid thickly timbered forests. The emu, along with the kangaroo, is featured on the Australian Coat of Arms.

Grey Butcherbird (Above)
The male and female grey butcherbirds (*Cracticus torquatus*) have the same appearance and colouring. They are abundant throughout wooded regions and feed primarily on insects, lizards, fruit, seeds and occasionally smaller birds. Notable characteristics include their fierce protection of their nest and chicks, and their enchanting musical song, often sung alternately.

Satin Bowerbird (Left)
Luring a female to his domain is the satin bowerbird (*Ptilonorhynchus violaceus*). The bower bird is so named because the male constructs a bower (which is quite separate from the nest) from erect twigs and sticks which he decorates with objects, mostly blue in colour, such as flowers, shells or litter. During the breeding season, the male performs an elaborate courtship display here in order to attract the olive-green female. Bowerbirds inhabit rainforest regions from Victoria to eastern Queensland.

Woodhen (Right)
Bantam-sized and flightless, the rare woodhen (*Tricholimnas sylvestris*) is only found on Lord Howe Island. This rare bird was on the verge of extinction in 1980; only 23 individuals were alive but now, after an extensive breeding programme funded by the National Parks and Wildlife Foundation, a recent census revealed some 150 birds are alive and thriving. The woodhen has a strong beak with which it forages for food through the forest litter.

Southern Cassowary (Left)
Peculiar and helmeted, the southern cassowary (*Casuarius casuarius*) is a huge, flightless bird which thrives in the dimly lit tropical rainforests of north-eastern Queensland. The female is larger and more richly coloured than the male, who incubates and cares for the young up to nine months after they hatch. The female's only participation is in laying the four bright green eggs. Cassowarys make a low, throaty, rumbling sound when approached and feed primarily on fallen fruits and dead birds within the rainforest.

Gang-Gang Cockatoo (Right)
Mountain forests and densely wooded areas of south-eastern Australia are the habitats favoured by the friendly gang-gang cockatoo (*Callocephalon fimbriatum*). During the breeding season, from October to January, the birds remain in pairs. The male's general plumage is grey with a head and crest of bright red, while the female's plumage is patterned with white bars. Like most cockatoos, they primarily feed on seeds and nuts of native trees which they crack open with their strong bills.

Australian Pelican (Below)
Conspicuous, popular and abundant, the Australian pelican (*Pelecanus conspicillatus*) is often seen all over the continent where there is water; lakes, swamps, estuaries and the ocean. Pelicans are accomplished flyers even though take-off and landing is sometimes clumsy, and with webbed feet are expert swimmers. Their huge pink bill is the perfect fish trap, enabling them to efficiently catch their diet of fish and crustaceans.

Barn Owl (Above)
The charming, round-faced barn owl (*Tyto alba*) is nocturnal; active throughout the night-time and sedentary during the day, when it often retreats to trees, caves or farm buildings. Living alone or in pairs, these birds favour open-wooded regions or farming areas where a food supply of mice and rodents is abundant. Both sexes are similar in colour and appearance.

Pink Cockatoo (Above)
The pink cockatoo (*Cacatua leadbeateri*) is more frequently referred to as Major Mitchell's cockatoo, named after the explorer Sir Thomas Mitchell who was very much impressed by this beautiful bird. Central Australia, the arid and semi-arid areas, is the pink cockatoos' home where they spend most of their time on the ground feeding on seeds, nuts, fruits and roots. They nest in hollow tree branches and trunks, from August to December, where the chicks stay for about six weeks.

Pied Heron (Right)
Sometimes called the white-headed egret, even though it has a black head, the pied heron (*Ardea picata*) is a stately wading bird that frequents tropical saltwater and freshwater swamps of northern Australia. These herons breed throughout the year, building platform nests of sticks and twigs in which three to four blue-green eggs are laid. They eat an enormous range of insects and other invertebrates.

Darter (Above)
Often called the snake-bird because of its long, slender neck, the darter (*Anhinga melanogaster*) is an accomplished flyer as well as an excellent swimmer; it totally submerges its body underneath the water with only the head and neck protruding above the surface. Darters live anywhere there is water and an abundant food supply of fish and crustaceans, which they spear with their sharp-pointed bill.

Sulphur-Crested Cockatoo (Left)
Probably the best-known of Australian birds is the handsome sulphur-crested cockatoo (*Cacatua galerita*). These familiar, ubiquitous birds are extremely noisy; their loud, continuous screeching can be heard long before they are seen. Seeds, berries and nuts are their favourite food which they crack open with their powerful beaks. Unfortunately these large birds are often caged as pets.

Plumed Pigeon (Right)
The male and female plumed pigeon (*Petrophassa plumifera*) are alike in colour and appearance. Also called spinifex pigeons, the arid desert areas of the central and northern part of the country provide their permanent home. After rain, rapidly growing plants produce an abundant seed crop on which the birds feed.

Rainbow Lorikeet (Above)
Gregarious, conspicuous, brilliantly coloured and extremely noisy, the rainbow lorikeet (*Trichoglossus haematodus*) inhabits forested areas along the east coast. Greedily, these delightful birds feed on nectar, pollen, blossoms, berries and seeds; often travelling in flocks of hundreds. These infectiously happy birds are one of our favourite parrots.

Eastern Rosella (Left)
One of our best known parrots is the gregarious and abundant eastern rosella (*Platycercus eximius*). Favouring the lightly timbered portions of the eastern coastline, where an ample feast of grass, seeds, blossoms, nectar, fruit and insects is available, these vividly plumaged birds nest in the hollow of a tree from August to January. The female incubates the four to seven eggs and cares for the young.

Tawny Frogmouth (Right)
A clever exponent of camouflage, the tawny frogmouth (*Podargus strigoides*) blends well into the trees and branches in which it sits motionlessly during the day. Being nocturnal, these birds spend the night hours searching for food. They fly silently and slowly. Males and females are uniform in colour and appearance.

Superb Lyrebird (Left, above and below)
Shy, cautious and elusive the superb lyrebird (*Menura novaehollandiae*) dwells in the dimly lit, damp gullies of wet forests in south-eastern Australia. Unlike the female, the male has a beautiful lyre-shaped tail which he spreads in a fan-like manner forward over his head, softly shaking it to attract a mate. Interestingly, a male may mate with several different females during June and July and he doesn't participate in nest-building or care of the one offspring. Another peculiarity is the lyrebird's ability to expertly mimic the calls of other birds and sometimes even human sounds.

Port Lincoln Ringneck (Below)
Like most parrots, the Port Lincoln ringneck (*Barnardius zonarius*) is boisterous and inquisitive. Copious throughout timbered zones of the south-western part of the country, pairs nest in the hollow of a tree branch and feed on plant foliage. Both sexes are alike in appearance.

Dollarbird (Above)
The dark, large, richly coloured and stout dollarbird (*Eurystomus orientalis*) is basically tropical, spending winter in New Guinea then flying south to the northern regions of Australia during the breeding months of spring. The female is duller and paler than the male and both feed primarily on large insects.

Rufous Whistler (Above right)
Feeding two hungry chicks is the rufous whistler (*Pachycephala rufiventris*). Abundant in all open forests throughout the entire country, this happy little songster has an enchanting and loud chorus which often signifies the onset of spring. An intricate cup-shaped nest of twigs and grasses is woven during the breeding time from September to February and the birds mostly feed on small insects.

Yellow-Faced Honeyeater (Right above)
Breeding from July to March, raising two or three chicks, the yellow-faced honeyeater (*Lichenostomus chrysops*) inhabits the forest, woodland and mangrove regions of eastern Australia. Hordes of flocks fly north from South Australia and Victoria into New South Wales and Queensland during autumn then return again in spring. Abundant and active, the males and females are similiar in size and appearance.

Striated Thornbill (Right)
Tiny and delicate, the striated thornbill (*Acanthiza lineata*) grows to a length of only about 100 mm. An oval-shaped nest of slender bark and grasses secured by spiderweb is constructed high in the trees of wet and dry forest regions of south-eastern Australia. Usually three young are raised.

White-Throated Warbler (Below)

Elaborately woven, the dome-shaped hanging nest created out of bark strips bound with spiderweb and lined with feathers takes the male and female white-throated warbler (*Gerygone olivacea*) eleven to fourteen days to assemble. Both sexes are similar in appearance and reside in the open eucalypt woodlands of the coastal fringes of the country.

Little Penguin (Below right)

Often called the fairy penguin, the little penguin (*Eudyptula minor*) is the smallest of the eighteen species of penguins and is the only one to breed in Australia. It is seen most commonly on Phillip Island near Melbourne. These flightless birds are proficient swimmers, making good use of their wings as flippers and their webbed feet. They have short, stiff feathers under which a thick layer of down acts as insulation to their bodies. Males and females are uniform in appearance.

Plumed Whistling-Duck (Right)

The handsome plumed whistling-duck (*Dendrocygna eytoni*) occupies the tropical grassland areas near swamps and lagoons, gradually moving towards the wetter coast during the dry season. During the tropical wet spell birds mate and often form a lifelong partnership. Both sexes are similar in plumage and size and participate in nest-building, incubation of the eight to fourteen eggs and care of the young.

Green Catbird (Above)
Strikingly elegant, the green catbird (*Ailuroedus crassirostris*) is so named because of its cat-like cry, which is called to mark its territory. Shy and elusive, the catbird rarely leaves its rainforest home of the central and south-eastern coast. Travelling singly or in pairs, males and females are alike and eat fruit and leaves.

White-Capped Noddy (Above right)
Inhabiting the islands off the Queensland coast, the white-capped noddy (*Anous minutus*) picks its diet of fish, molluscs, cuttlefish, jellyfish and plankton from the water with its sharply pointed bill. Sleekly plumaged, both sexes are identical in appearance and breed from August to January, rearing only one chick.

White Ibis (Right)
Feeding its young here, the white ibis (*Threskiornis molucca*) breeds from September to December constructing a platform nest of sticks and twigs lined with aquatic foliage. Male and female birds are similar and oddly they have no feathers on their black head or neck. Residing in the swampy waterways of the northern and eastern half of the country, these graceful fliers often take wing in a V-shaped formation. Mainly feeding in the water their diet consists of fish, crustaceans, frogs and insects.

Royal Spoonbill (Above)
The tall, regal wader, the royal spoonbill (*Platalea regia*), is so called because of its long, spoon-shaped bill. This well-adapted bill is used effectively to catch mainly fish as the bird wades through the shallow waters of lagoons and marshes. These nomadic birds always dwell near water; marine or fresh. During breeding time, the male collects the nest-building materials of sticks and twigs, while the female constructs the nest. Later the eggs will be incubated by each parent alternately.

Buff-Banded Rail (Left)
Dwelling around coastal watercourses, wet grasslands, lagoons and thickly vegetated swamps, the buff-banded rail (*Rallus philippensis*) is a timid and rarely seen bird that will run quickly when disturbed even though it can fly. Attractively plumaged, both sexes look similar. Their diet mostly consists of insects, molluscs and seeds found in and near their aquatic habitat. Breeding throughout most of the year these waterbirds rear about five to eleven young.

Blue-Winged Kookaburra (Right)
Being the closest relative to the laughing kookaburra, the blue-winged kookaburra (*Dacelo leachii*) often shares the same habitat as its counterpart and they have many similar characteristics. Male and female birds are alike but the male has a brilliant deep-blue tail and rump whereas the female has a brown-striped tail. These gregarious, raucous and infectiously happy birds live in tropical woodlands of the north-eastern coastal fringes and the northern sector of the continent from Western Australia right across the top to Queensland.

Budgerigar (Above)
Probably the most abundant and best known of the Australian parrots is the little, chattering budgerigar (*Melopsittacus undulatus*) one of the world's most popular cage birds. It is very nomadic as it wanders the open plains of central Australia in search of grass seed and water. Males and females are alike in appearance and nest annually in the hollow of a tree, log or even a fence post where they raise four to six chicks.

Galah (Right)
One of our most beautiful parrots is the well-known and copious galah (*Cacatua roseicapilla*). Often seen in large flocks distributed throughout savannah woodlands and open grasslands over most of the continent, except the farthest east coast, the south-western corner and Tasmania, they gregariously gather seeds from the ground. Breeding adults return to the same nesting site, a tree hollow lined with eucalypt leaves, year after year.

Flora

Australia's beautiful and unequalled plantlife is envied and renowned worldwide. Magnificent trees and shrubs, and colourful flowers grow prolifically throughout the entire expanse of the continent even though the majority are most particular in their requirements. Their robustness and healthiness depends entirely on the environment in which they grow—the soil quality, terrain, climate and most importantly the availability of water.

One-third of our country lies north of the Tropic of Capricorn therefore the climate is dominantly tropical and warm-temperate. Coastal fringes are well moistened by the ocean and sea-breezes therefore lush, dense and rich vegetation is found thriving here, particularly along the eastern coastline. Travelling inland from the seaboard, weather and geographic conditions gradually alter—the further towards the centre of the country one goes, the hotter, drier and more desolate the landscape becomes. The plantlife becomes more sparse, tougher and more tolerant. It has evolved to survive the parched desert interior.

Much endemic flora is abundant. Because Australia evolved over an extensive period of time and in total isolation, well-adapted vegetation developed to perfectly suit the environment.

Australian flora flourishes in its particular positions and landscapes. Some of the many different vegetation categories which are predominant and vigorous throughout our country are described below.

Rainforests

Along the well-watered east coastline from Cape York in far northern Queensland down to Tasmania, dense, lush rainforests flourish in these very high-rainfall regions. Colossal trees, more than 30 metres tall, such as the booyong, giant stinging tree and the red cedar, tower majestically forming a thick canopy which allows very little light to penetrate. Palms, vines, ferns, orchids, tree-ferns, staghorns, elkhorns, fungi and mosses thrive within the wet leaf litter of the forest floor and in the evergreen, moist conditions. Interestingly, there are more species of plantlife within the realms of rainforest than in any other plant community.

Subtropical rainforests

Even though the number of rainforest species may be less here than in other rainforest types and the canopy height only stands at about 10 to 27 metres, subtropical rainforests often support a greater diversity of ferns, mosses and palms, such as the Bangalow.

Temperate rainforests

Occurring in moist tracts of Tasmania and along the east coast of the mainland to as far as Queensland, temperate rainforests are usually dominated by one species of tree, such as the Antarctic beech. Like other rainforests, many tree-ferns, lichens and mosses also flourish.

Open Forests

Sclerophyll (hard-leafed) forests or open forests dominate the Australian terrain. Towering, straight-trunked eucalyptus trees prosper in the evergreen sectors of the higher rainfall areas of Victoria, Tasmania, New South Wales and Queensland. The wet sclerophyll forests of coastal fringes, tableland districts of the south-eastern and south-western part of the mainland as well as much of Tasmania, are dominated by exceptionally tall trees often reaching more than 60 metres. Much light filters through an open canopy allowing smaller trees, shrubs, tree-ferns, ground ferns and grasses to grow copiously. Dry sclerophyll forests are common in less fertile regions on the coast and tablelands. Most commonly, these forests consist of two species of eucalypts, usually less than 30 metres in height. Numerous varieties of shrubs abound.

Woodlands

Dominated by evergreen eucalypts and occasionally by casuarinas, melaleucas or acacia trees, these forests thrive in the drier parts of the inland zones of our country, from the Kimberleys in Western Australia, across the Northern Territory into the central areas of Queensland, New South Wales and Victoria. Woodlands are probably our most recognisable plant communities; they boast an enormous assortment of low-growing trees, shrubs, herbs, creepers, grasses and colourful flowering plants. Types of woodland include tropical, subtropical, temperate, subhumid, alpine, semi-arid and arid. Many Australian bird species live in these regions where the density of tree cover can vary from almost forests to sparse woodlands that are almost grasslands.

Scrublands

As the name implies, scrubland is made up of dense, scrubby growth with low-growing trees (usually less than 8 metres in height) that form a light canopy.

Mallee scrubland grows in the arid and semi-arid regions containing several species of low-growing eucalypts which have many trunks growing out of the one swollen base. Acacia scrubland is also prevalent in these arid regions where rainfall is less than 550 mm per year.

Grasslands

Obviously, areas dominated by grasses are called grasslands. These mostly treeless regions cover about 23 per cent of our land, mostly the arid zones. Arid tussock or spinifex landscapes usually have no trees and occur in western Queensland and eastern Northern Territory while other grasslands such as alpine, swamp, those of the south-east highlands and around the northern tropical coastline fill the remainder.

Alpine Regions

These areas are very limited in our country due to the low mountain ranges. Our highest point, Mt Koscuisko in New South Wales, is only 2228 metres, so alpine flora is noticeably confined. During the cold winter months snow covers the higher peaks, but during January and February colourful flowering annuals and herbaceous plants, such as the snow daisy and mountain gentians perform a dazzling display. The twisted-trunked snow gum is prolific throughout the sub-alpine zone.

Heathlands

Small, evergreen, hard-leafed shrubs inhabit the infertile soils of coastal regions and sandy plains from far northern Queensland, along the eastern coastline as far south as Tasmania and across to the south-west of Western Australia. Low-growing shrubs and plants are amongst the most colourful including heaths, wattles, bottlebrushes and banksias.

Mangroves

Strong arching roots of mangroves help anchor these trees firmly in the mud of river estuaries and bays of the northern and eastern coastline of Australia. Mangroves reach up these waterways as far as the tidal limit extends.

Wetlands

Partly due to Australia's flat topography, substantially developed wetlands are few and far between. Northern rivers swell and flood annually during the heavy rains of the wet season, so many lagoons and swamps are temporarily formed on the river floodplains but the dry season quickly follows and most of this water evaporates. More permanent swamps and lagoons are found in eastern Queensland, and the south-east and south-west regions of the continent. Aquatic foliage includes water hyacinths, various reeds and rushes.

Deserts

The harsh desert interior of our continent is hot, dry and desolate apart from the low, stunted shrubs, saltbushes, tussock grasses and spinifex that sparsely grow and survive there. After rain, however, a carpet of colourful annuals and perennials blossoms bringing life to these seemingly barren and lifeless landscapes.

Heathland
Exposed to the open sea, coastal heathland on the eastern side of the continent is abundant in hardy, low-growing shrubs and a variety of flowering plants that comfortably tolerate their windy, sea-blown existence.

Desert (Above, and right, above and below)
The desert inland of Australia is an arid landscape—dry, sparsely vegetated with spinifex, tough shrubs and diminutive trees. But after rain, annual grasses, flowering plants and new growth bring this seemingly desolate region to life.

Rainforests (Left, right and below)
Rainforests thrive in the high rainfall regions along the east coast from Cape York to Tasmania. Giant trees, such as the booyong, red cedar and black apple form a dense canopy which obliterates sunlight from the moist forest floor. Under this tree-top awning, orchids, ferns, mosses and fungi prosper in the constantly damp environment. (Crator National Park, Queensland)

Mangroves (Above)
Mangrove trees of northern Queensland have a vast network of breathing roots which occasionally become totally submerged in the tidal, muddy and swampy areas in which they flourish.

Dry Sclerophyll Forest (Right)
Dominated by large, evergreen eucalypts, with their tall, straight trunks, dry sclerophyll forests are established in the average rainfall areas. Smaller trees, shrubs, ferns and grasses grow profusely in the ample sunlight allowed onto the forest floor.

Alpine (Left and below)
Snow gums (*Eucalyptus niphophila*) are a major botanic feature of the alpine expanse around Mt Kosciusko. Below 1850 metres vegetation is varied yet sparse but in summer a host of colourful flowers bloom over the entire exposed landscape.

Christmas Bells (Right)
From late December to February, the moist east-coast heathlands erupt with the brightly coloured Christmas bells (*Blandfordia* sp.). Stiff stems carrying the red and yellow bell-shaped flowers arise about 75 cm from the grass-like leaves of the plant.

Cootamundra Wattle (Left)
Australia's floral emblem is the brilliantly colourful Cootamundra wattle (*Acacia baileyana*). Over five hundred kinds of wattle, greatly diverse in size, shape and colour, flourish throughout the country. Soft, fluffy, puff-ball flowers appear ranging in shades from light yellow, gold to deep orange.

Albany or Swamp Daisy (Right)
A small, densely flowering shrub, the Albany or swamp daisy (*Actinodium cunninghamii*) is only found in the south-west corner of Western Australia. Exquisite daisy flowers bloom profusely during spring.

Baobab (Below)
Bottle-shaped, squat and bloated, the baobab (*Adansonia gregorii*) is native to the top end of our country from northern Western Australia across the Kimberleys to the Northern Territory. The huge trunk, which may be as wide as 20 metres, holds extensive amounts of water enabling this deciduous tree to survive prolonged dry spells.

***Eucalyptus* sp.** (Left, above and right)
About 600 species of *Eucalyptus* are found mainly in Australia; some grow in New Guinea and South-East Asia. Gum trees, as they are often called, grow in an enormous variety of areas and fluctuate from stunted, twisted shrubs to towering, straight-trunked forest giants.

Eucalypt blossoms lack sepals and petals and like most flowers, the stamens of white, yellow, pink or red form a colourful display providing food for many native birds and mammals. Before opening, each gum flower is covered by a cap called an 'operculum' and this is discarded when the bloom opens.

The gumnut is formed after the flower dies—the floral tube, containing seeds, hardens, changes colour and opens, spilling the seeds onto the earth.

Flannel Flower (Above left)
Blooming during spring and summer throughout New South Wales and Queensland, the delicate flannel flower (*Actinotus helianthi*) has soft, flannel-like creamy-white flowers, each petal tipped with green.

Waratah (Left)
With its spectacular red flowers, the waratah (*Telopea speciosissima*) is the floral emblem of New South Wales. A hardy bush that grows to about 2 metres, it has tough, dark green, serrated leaves and is superb when in bloom during spring.

Pink Mulla Mulla (Above)
Commonly called pink mulla mulla, this member of the *Ptilotus* species grows in the warm, dry inland areas of Western Australia. Soft and fluffy white, pink or purple flowers cover the leaves and stems.

Heath (Above)
About thirty different kinds of heaths grow throughout this country, except in the Northern Territory and Western Australia. The native fuchsia *(Epacris longiflora)* has attractive, hanging, tubular flowers that sprout from the thin stems which are covered in small, sharply pointed leaves.

Banksias (Left, above and below)
Banksias were named after the botanist, Sir Joseph Banks. Of the fifty or so species, which are mainly restricted to Western Australia, the striking scarlet banksia (*Banksia coccinea*) is one of the most stunning varieties flowering throughout autumn to spring.

Green Kangaroo Paw (Right)
Resembling the claw of the marsupial after which it was named, the unusual green kangaroo paw (*Anigozanthos* sp.) is native to Western Australia. Green, red or yellow flowers bloom at the end of long, stiff stems which are often up to a metre in length.

Dendrobium kingianum (Left)
Another of the dendrobiums is the beautiful pink *Dendrobium kingianum.*

Sarchochilus falcatus (Right)
Widely known as the orange blossom orchid, the dainty blooms of *Sarchochilus falcatus* flower white, cream and, rarely, pale pink. This is a member of the rather small genus of orchids which is represented by about twelve species in Australia.

Phalaenopsis amabilis (Below)
This exquisitely beautiful white bloom belongs to a very rare species of orchid found only in northern rainforests of Queensland. This species is *Phalaenopsis amabilis* and each flower opens to about 7 cm in diameter.

Bottlebrush (Above)
Undoubtedly one of the best known and most widely grown of our flora is the bottlebrush (*Callistemon* sp.). Profuse white, pink, yellow, mauve, red or crimson flowers bloom on these hardy, bushy shrubs during spring to autumn, attracting flocks of native birds.

Fringed Lily (Right)
Exquisitely delicate and softly fringed, the dainty three-petalled fringed lily (*Thysanotus tuberosus*) is a perennial herb that bears beautiful purple flowers. It is found in all States except Tasmania.

Dendrobium tetragonum (Above left)
This spidery-looking orchid, *Dendrobium tetragonum*, is one of about sixty species of dendrobium growing in Australia. The majority of these are epiphytes found growing on trees while only a few thrive on rocks. Most are tropical and subtropical.

Sturt's Desert Pea (Left)
South Australia's State emblem is the exceptional Sturt's desert pea (*Clianthus formosus*). Growing immediately after rain, the stems and leaves are covered with soft, fine hairs and the unusual scarlet and black flowers appear during spring and summer.

Bushfire (Overleaf)
Bushfires are a devastating yet vital factor in the life of the Australian bush. Seed pods are burnt, become dry and drop their contents to the blackened floor where they germinate and grow, replenishing the charred landscape. Sadly, many fauna species are trapped in the sweeping infernos and often perish.

Reptiles and Amphibians

Reptiles and amphibians have been included in one section because even though at first appearance they may seem quite dissimilar, they are, in fact, closely related and share many common characteristics and ancestral bonds.

Reptiles

Of the 6000 living species of reptiles found throughout the world today, approximately 530 species have been described in Australia. Of these, there are about 110 species of snakes, 400 species of lizards, 2 species of crocodiles and 21 species of tortoises and turtles.

Reptiles occupy an important niche on the evolutionary tree. They first appeared during the Carboniferous Period over 280 million years ago, being the link between amphibians and the warm-blooded vertebrates, namely birds and mammals.

All reptiles are cold-blooded (ectothermic) which means their body temperature is regulated by their environment. They depend on their surroundings to provide the warmth they need to absorb body heat. They are vertebrates and are air-breathing. They do not possess hairs or feathers but instead their body covering is one of dry, scaly skin with few or no glands.

They typically reproduce by the female laying leathery-shelled eggs, but some are viviparous, which means they bear live young. The parental care of the eggs and infants is quite minimal. Reptiles have successfully adapted to all parts of Australia—deserts, grasslands, forests, swamps and rivers.

Most are harmless unless provoked. At the first recognition of danger most scurry away—snakes and lizards slither under a rock or into long grass, turtles and crocodiles submerge themselves in water and sink out of sight.

Snakes

Interestingly, Australia is the only place in the world in which the number of venomous snake species is greater than non-venomous species. However, snakes only pose a danger to man if interferred with or cornered.

Snakes have no legs but can efficiently and swiftly move by a succession of muscular body movements. They are carnivorous, eating small mammals, birds, rodents, amphibians and other reptiles.

There are about 110 species of snakes in Australia including two of the world's most deadly inhabitants, the taipan and the tiger snake.

Lizards

While there are many venomous Australian snakes, there are no poisonous lizards in this country—all are quite harmless even though some, like the goanna, can inflict a painful bite.

Most lizards are four-legged (quadrupedal), however there is one species of legless lizard.

Characteristically, most lizards are carnivorous, eating amphibians, insects, and small reptiles but some are herbivorous, eating plant foliage.

The lizard family includes geckos, monitors, goannas, skinks and the legless lizards.

Crocodiles

These ancient-looking monsters are the closest living relatives of the dinosaurs. Although probably the most ferocious of our reptiles, like snakes, if respected and left undisturbed, crocodiles pose no threat or danger to man.

Of the twenty-one species worldwide, two species occur in Australia—the freshwater or Johnston crocodile and the estuarine or salt-water crocodile.

Crocodiles have webbed toes evolved for their aquatic lifestyle; their back is covered in horny plates called scutes. Females prepare nests near the riverbank into which they lay from twenty to seventy eggs.

They are carnivorous, eating mammals, insects, molluscs, birds, frogs, fish and other reptiles.

Tortoises and Turtles

Of the some twenty-one species of tortoises and turtles found in Australia, fifteen species are freshwater and six are marine. Tortoises are usually freshwater while turtles prefer saltwater environments.

A hard shell protects their soft body and only allows their limbs, head and tail to protrude. When threatened they retreat into this permanent abode.

These slow-moving reptiles are accomplished swimmers and water is essential for their survival. They feed primarily on molluscs, insects and crustaceans but eat very little fish. The female lays her eggs in huge holes scooped out in the sand. Here they incubate and the young hatchlings begin their struggle to the water to start life unaided by their parents.

Amphibians

Amphibians occupy the position between fishes and reptiles on the evolutionary tree. They were the first to venture from a totally aquatic environment onto land; they developed lungs and legs enabling them to become in part terrestrial, and so became the forefathers of reptiles, birds and mammals.

The oldest amphibian fossil is dated at about 370 million years. Amphibians are believed to have evolved from fishes during the Devonian Period developing into 'terrestrial fishes' able to breathe air via mouth and lungs. Understandably, there are fewer species of amphibians than any other land-dwelling vertebrate class.

Like reptiles, amphibians are vertebrate and cold-blooded (ectothermic) and have no hair or feathers, but they don't have scales either. Instead, they possess a soft, moist, glandular skin which is smooth and scaleless and susceptible to drying out. This is why it is essential for them to live near water or moisture.

Nearly all amphibian species live part of their lives on land, either under moist vegetation or near creeks, rivers or waterholes; very few live an entirely aquatic existence.

The female usually lays her shell-less eggs in water where they remain and develop through a larval stage. Tadpoles (aquatic larvae) metamorphose (transform) into terrestrial adults who live near water. There are about 2400 living species of amphibians in the world today and approximately 188 have been found in Australia.

This interesting group includes the frogs, toads and salamanders.

Copperhead Snake (Below)
Frequenting rivers, creeks and swamps of the coastal areas of New South Wales, Victoria, south-east South Australia and Tasmania, the copperhead snake (*Austrelaps superbus*) eats frogs, small mammals, lizards, snakes and is highly cannibalistic—eating other members of its own species. Colour may vary from black, brown to tan and the female is viviparous, producing about twenty live young. This snake measures about one and a half metres and is very venomous thus is extremely dangerous to humans.

Common Death Adder (Above)
Averaging a length of 38 to 50 cm, the broad, thick common death adder (*Acanthophis antarcticus*) varies in colour from light grey, dark grey, reddish-brown to dark brown. Favouring sandy, low-foliaged locations, a female can produce up to ten or fifteen live young. Especially active on warm evenings, these nocturnal reptiles feed on rodents, birds and lizards. They are aggressive, striking swiftly and accurately and are highly venomous and dangerous to humans.

Bandy-Bandy (Left)
Common throughout the entire country and particularly widespread in New South Wales, the easily recognised black-and-white-striped bandy-bandy (*Vermicella annulata*) lives in sandy environments. This nocturnal snake eats blind snakes and small lizards and the female can lay up to six eggs. Even though it is venomous it is unlikely to be harmful to humans.

Amethystine Python (Below left)
Often called the scrub python, the amethystine python (*Morelia amethistina*) is the largest python living in Australia. Inhabiting the tropical rainforests of north-eastern Queensland, this snake averages 4.5 metres in length, but a specimen has been recorded measuring some 7.5 metres. Basically nocturnal, it eats small mammals and birds and even though non-venomous can cause a very painful bite. The female lays ten to twenty eggs.

Burton's Legless Lizard (Right)
With a body pattern and colour that can vary greatly, Burton's legless lizard (*Lialis burtonis*) can easily be distinguished by its long, pointed snout. These lizards may grow to about 60 cm in length. They eat small lizards and are most active during the night.

Bearded Dragon (Left)
Ferocious-looking, yet quite harmless, the bearded dragon (*Amphibolurus barbatus*) opens its yellow-lined mouth, stands puffed-out and spreads out its beard when threatened. Common throughout the eastern half of the continent, excluding Tasmania and the far north, it eats insects, worms, rodents, small lizards and its favourite herb, dandelion. The female may lay up to as many as twenty-five eggs and adults average 75 cm in length.

Salt-Water Crocodile (Below left)
Living in the briny waters and ocean from the Kimberleys across to Queensland, the largest of our reptiles is the salt-water crocodile (*Crocodylus porosus*). It is one of only two species found in Australia. Being the closest living relative to the extinct dinosaurs, this carnivorous animal is an accomplished swimmer aided by webbed feet and its mighty, propulsive tail. Specimens have been recorded at reaching a length of 7 metres however over 5 metres is rare. Usually nocturnal in its habits, the crocodile feeds on mammals, birds, reptiles, fish and crustaceans, often drowning its prey. During the breeding months, a female lays about sixty eggs which hatch after three to five months.

Lace Monitor (Below)
Prehistoric in appearance, the lace monitor (*Varanus varius*) is commonly called a tree goanna and is our second-largest lizard, growing up to a length of some 2 metres. Inhabiting the forested localities from the far north-eastern edge of Queensland through the coastal and inland regions of New South Wales to Victoria and South Australia, lace monitors primarily feast on birds, rodents, small mammals, reptiles, carrion and eggs. Female monitors are oviparous, usually laying six eggs per clutch.

Common Tree Snake (Above)
The non-venomous, slender and agile common tree snake (*Dendrelaphis punctulatus*) is dexterous among trees as well as on the ground and in the water. Averaging a length of about 1.25 metres, these reptiles feast on frogs, geckoes and skinks found in their habitat throughout north-western Australia.

Pink-Tongued Lizard (Above)
Dwelling in rock clefts or in the bark of trees, the pink-tongued lizard (*Tiliqua gerrardii*) ranges in coastal rainforests from far northern Queensland south to the central coast of New South Wales. Mostly nocturnal, and particularly active on balmy evenings, these harmless reptiles consume almost exclusively snails and slugs. During the breeding season a female may produce up to twenty-four live young.

Children's Python (Above right)
Frequenting rocky regions of the Northern Territory, Western Australia, South Australia, Queensland and New South Wales, the harmless children's python (*Liasis childreni*) grows to an average length of 1.25 metres. Like most snakes, it is nocturnal in habit feeding on lizards, frogs, small mammals and sometimes small birds.

Eastern Water Dragon (Right above)
Often lolling on exposed rocks or a tree branch, the semi-aquatic eastern water dragon (*Physignathus lesueurii*) resides along waterways of the east coast from far northern Queensland right down to southern New South Wales.

Eastern Snake-Necked Tortoise (Right)
One of the most familiar of reptiles is the eastern snake-necked tortoise (*Chelodina longicollis*). Averaging a length of only 20 cm, these reptiles are distributed from Queensland, inland and coastal New South Wales, down to Victoria and South Australia. Breeding during the spring and summer months, a female lays about eight to twenty-four eggs in the soil and the young emerge between January and February.

Ring-Tailed Dragon (Right)
Extremely diverse in colouration, varying from fawn, to orange-brown to vivid brick-red, the ring-tailed dragon (*Amphibolurus caudicinctus*) inhabits sectors of far western Queensland through the Northern Territory into northern South Australia and the greater part of Western Australia. One of our fastest-moving lizards, the male is larger in frame than the female, often reaching a length of some 28 cm.

Cunningham's Skink (Left)
Basking in the warm sunshine is a Cunningham's skink (*Egernia cunninghami*) which thrives in the rocky regions from south-eastern Queensland, across New South Wales into Victoria and South Australia. Reaching a length of about 45 cm, these very sociable reptiles often live in large colonies and flourish on a diet of insects, worms, snails and ground vegetation.

Blue-Tongued Lizard (Below left)
Often noticed in urban gardens, the slow-moving and harmless blue-tongued lizard (*Tiliqua scincoides*) is so named because of its vivid blue tongue. Growing to an average length of 50 cm, the lizards dine on snails, insects, fruit and mice. The female is viviparous—bearing about ten live young.

Red-Bellied Black Snake (Below)
Preferring the moist environments around rivers, swamps, lakes or watercourses, the sleek, glossy, red-bellied black snake (*Pseudechis porphyriacus*) averages a length of 1.25 metres and being venomous is dangerous to humans. Distributed throughout the eastern zones from far northern Queensland, into New South Wales, Victoria and south-eastern South Australia, this diurnal snake feasts on frogs, reptiles and small mammals during the daylight hours and the female bears eight to forty live young.

Green Turtle (Above and left)
Somewhat cumbersome on land but agile in the warm tropical waters along the northern fringes of our country and the Great Barrier Reef, the attractive green turtle (*Chelonia mydas*) is almost entirely herbivorous. The female lays about one hundred eggs into a sand cavity where they incubate and hatch.

Diamond Python (Right above)
Appropriately named, the diamond python (*Morelia spilota spilotes*) is one of our most ornate and beautifully embellished snakes. Common throughout the mainland, except in the dry desert interior, southern Victoria and the far west, this harmless large reptile averages a length of 2 metres and mostly dines on small land vertebrates. During the breeding time a female lays ten to twenty eggs per clutch, often coiling around them to aid in incubation.

Black Rock Skink (Right)
Dwelling in rocky nooks and crannies of highland regions of south-eastern Australia from western Victoria to south-eastern areas of Queensland, the scarce black rock skink (*Egernia saxatilis*) grows to a length of some 30 cm and feasts on worms and insects.

***Neobatrachus* sp.** (Above left)
Typical of their species, *Neobatrachus*, these small rotund burrowing frogs have a warty skin that is rough in texture and covered with dark olive-green blotches.

Northern Banjo Frog (Below left)
This dumpy yet smartly coloured northern banjo frog (*Limnodynastes terraereginae*) can be found around swamps, estuaries and farm dams throughout the western parts of northern New South Wales, across eastern Queensland right up to the Cape York Peninsula.

(Above)
An attractive frog, this is another of the *Limnodynastes* species showing off its powerful and well-built limbs.

Ornate Burrowing Frog (Right)
Most active after rain, the ornate burrowing frog (*Limnodynastes ornatus*) flourishes throughout northern New South Wales, Queensland and the north-western zones of Western Australia and the Northern Territory. Preferring ever-moist conditions these stout frogs dwell from wet coastal areas into drier woodlands away from the seaboard.

Green Tree Frog (Left)
One of our most common and attractive amphibians is the handsome green tree frog (*Litoria caerulea*). Its soft, moist, bright green skin is offset by a white-coloured belly. These abundant frogs range from coastal fringes to the drier interior regions of north-western Western Australia, the Northern Territory, Queensland, South Australia and New South Wales.

Spotted Grass Frog (Below left)
The huge bulging eyes of the spotted grass frog (*Limnodynastes tasmaniensis*) survey its territory. Common throughout Tasmania, Victoria, eastern parts of South Australia into New South Wales and eastern Queensland, these pretty frogs are able to survive from the ever-moist coastal regions into the drier interior. Like all frogs they need constant moisture so always stay near lagoons, creeks or permanent waterholes.

Green and Golden Bell Frog (Below)
Prospering amongst wet vegetation on the edges of streams, swamps, lagoons and most permanent waterways, the highly aquatic green and golden bell frog (*Litoria aurea*) inhabits moist zones of eastern and south-eastern New South Wales and far eastern portions of Victoria.

(Right)
What an agile climber, another of the attractive *Litoria* species.

Index